Armchair Walks

G000075309

Horsham

Written and Illustrated
by the Artist

Patricia Hall

Published by Patricia Hall Pictures 2009
www.pathallpics.co.uk

Copyright ©2009 text and illustrations Patricia Hall

All rights reserved. No part of this publication may be reproduced, stored in a retrieval system or transmitted in any form or by any means without the prior permission of the copyright holder.

ISBN 978-0-9563308-0-2

Designed by: adovation.co.uk
Printed by: Crisp Litho Ltd

Introduction - A Brief History

Horsham is a market town beside the river Arun in the very heart of Sussex. It has a rich history, lovely old buildings, hidden walkways and a pretty town centre.

In geological times, about 140 million years ago, the climate was warm and wet and dinosaurs roamed the area. Iguanodon bones have been found, some right in the middle of the town. Dinosaur remains, including claws and teeth, may well have given rise to the dragon legends associated with nearby St Leonard's Forest.

Femur of Iguanadon in Horsham Museum. Discovered in 1840 under St Mark's Church by George Bax Holmes who lived in the Causeway.

Some 4,000 years ago, Bronze Age hunter-gatherers were already in the Horsham area. We know this because hundreds of flint arrowheads have been found.

Arrowheads in the Museum. The one on the right was dug up by a young girl on a Horsham allotment in 2009 and has been dated circa 1800 B.C.

Much more recently, about 1,000 years ago, there was a seasonal movement of stock along drove roads from the coast. Farmers brought their animals in spring to fresh pastures on the sandy heaths of the Weald. Horsham developed where one of these drove roads crossed the River Arun. The name 'Horsham' comes from 'Horse Meadow'; a place where horses, cattle and sheep could graze in clearings in the forest. A market for animals was established in the developing town and a substantial church was built for the growing community.

From the early 1300s, Horsham was one of the county towns of Sussex. Judges would arrive from London to try the prisoners held in the local jail. They came on horseback, in full ceremonial regalia, attracting much attention. They stayed in town and attended church on Sunday before carrying out their duties the next week.

Following their visit, public executions sometimes took place on Horsham Common and these drew large crowds. They became known as Horsham Hang Fairs. If there were no hangings, the populace could join in the humiliation of the unfortunates at the whipping post or stocks. This turned into something of a carnival with fairground booths and pedlars.

In the Middle Ages, Horsham benefited from the timber trade of the surrounding forests and local merchants built fine houses for themselves. Further prosperity came to the town in Elizabethan times with the development of the Wealden Iron Industry. Streams were dammed to make hammer ponds, blast furnaces were built to smelt the local iron ore and 'tilt hammers' beat out the molten iron, hence the name 'hammer pond'. Both the bellows for the furnaces and the hammers were powered by waterwheels. The forest around Horsham would have been a noisy, busy, dirty place at this time.

When Britain was at war with France, at the end of the 1700s, Horsham became a military town and barracks were built near the present cricket ground. Thousands of soldiers were quartered in the town and local shops and hostelries did a roaring trade. Horsham flourished and the Duke of Norfolk turned the dilapidated market house into a smart town hall.

Horsham – Causeway   Patricia Hall

CAUSEWAY. Horsham's architectural gem connects the market place to the church and a crossing point on the river Arun, as it did in medieval times.

After the Battle of Waterloo, in 1815, the regiments disappeared, the barracks were dismantled and the town had a brief period of decline. However, its fortunes were revived in Victorian times by the coaching trade and then the arrival of the railway in 1848.

Today, the town has expanded greatly. Many old buildings have inevitably disappeared to make way for modern shopping precincts and commercial premises. However, its centre is attractively pedestrianised with trees, floral displays and pavement cafés. Many lovely old houses have survived and this walk will take you down Horsham's 'hidden gem', the Causeway. You can explore medieval alleyways, examine buildings of architectural interest, admire modern sculptures and hopefully gain a little flavour of the town's history.

CARFAX. This view from the bandstand shows the war memorial and outdoor seating areas. The entrance to Swan Walk is below the clock. There are many attractive trees in the Carfax and at Christmas these are decorated with festive lighting. Markets are held here and, on occasions, there is a traditional funfair, complete with Ferris wheel, from where you can get a grand view over the rooftops of the town.

The Main Walk

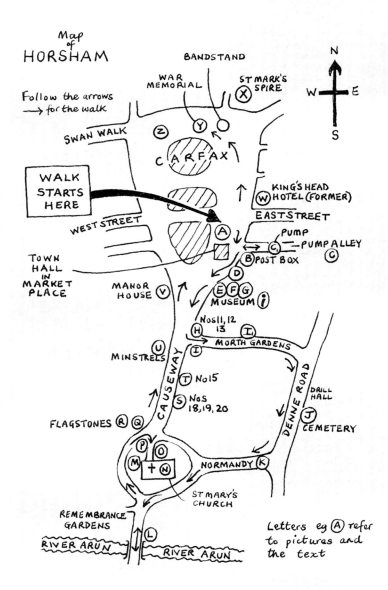

Map of HORSHAM

BANDSTAND

WAR MEMORIAL

ST MARK'S SPIRE

Follow the arrows → for the walk

SWAN WALK

Ⓩ Ⓨ ⓧ

CARFAX

WALK STARTS HERE

KING'S HEAD Ⓦ HOTEL (FORMER)

EAST STREET

WEST STREET

Ⓐ

PUMP
Ⓒ PUMP ALLEY
Ⓒ

Ⓑ POST BOX

TOWN HALL IN MARKET PLACE

MANOR HOUSE Ⓥ

Ⓓ
ⒺⒻⒼ
MUSEUM ⓘ

Nos 11, 12 13 Ⓘ
Ⓗ

MINSTRELS

Ⓤ

Ⓘ MORTH GARDENS

DRILL HALL

Ⓣ No 15

Ⓢ Nos 18, 19, 20

DENNE ROAD

Ⓙ CEMETERY

FLAGSTONES Ⓡ Ⓠ

CAUSEWAY

Ⓟ Ⓞ
Ⓜ ✝ Ⓝ

NORMANDY Ⓚ

ST MARY'S CHURCH

REMEMBRANCE GARDENS

Ⓛ

RIVER ARUN   RIVER ARUN

Letters eg Ⓐ refer to pictures and the text

6

A Walk Around Horsham

Park in any of the central car parks and make your way to the Town Hall which is in the SE corner of the Carfax. Duration: 1 to 1½ hours plus optional extension.

Picture A - TOWN HALL IN MARKET PLACE. The ground floor used to be an open arcade in which stalls were set up, hence its old name 'Market House'. The arches are now filled in. Notice the unusual castle-like crenellations and turrets.

The Town Hall (see map and picture A) is in Market Place. There has been a market building on this site since at least 1648. At one time the open arcaded ground floor was a market selling butter and poultry amongst other produce. The County Court sat on the upper floor and the judges often complained of the noise coming from below. There are still ten, small 'holding' cells in the basement where, in the 20th century, prisoners from the jail were held whilst awaiting their trial.

When the Duke of Norfolk rebuilt the Market House, in 1812, it became the Market and Town Hall and you can see his coat of arms on the front wall (with the Royal arms on the left and the arms of Horsham borough on the right). The clock was added in 1820 and then, in 1888, the Town Hall had a major refit, but the front was left intact.

In 1949, the infamous John George Haigh appeared before magistrates in this building charged with the Acid Bath Murders. He was committed for trial at Lewes.

Today, the ground floor is still used for markets but also for meetings and exhibitions. Horsham Registry Office is also here. The upper floor was the old council chamber. There are plans (2009) to change its use once again.

Ye Olde Post Box (B) is at the narrow entrance to Pump Alley just off Market Place. On the right was the Post Office. The letter box was really a hinged, wooden structure which opened so that you could hand your letters directly to the postmaster who sat behind. Here you can see and touch the medieval timbers of the old buildings on either side.

Picture B - YE OLDE POST BOX is in the narrow entrance to Pump Alley, just beside the Town Hall. This is the site of Horsham's first Post Office. This hinged panel opened so that letters could be handed in.

Picture C - PUMP ALLEY. In the corner, behind the wall, is a 20th century pump which gave its name to this narrow walkway from Market Place.

Pump Alley (C) is one of several narrow alleyways which led into the centre of the town from medieval times and it is still well preserved. The Talbot or Wonder Inn used to be on the left, hence its old name, Talbot Lane. A well with its pump once stood on the right of the alley, opposite the present one (C1).

Retrace your steps into Market Place and turn left into a delightful road called 'Causeway' or 'raised footway' which leads down to St Mary's Church. It was paved in the early 17th century and lime trees were planted in the mid 18th century. It thus became a fashionable and attractive avenue.

Picture C1 - PUMP. The original stood on the other side of the Alley.

Straight in front of you on the brick wall of number 8 Causeway is a wall plaque (D). Established in 1915, during the First World War, the War Hospital Supply Depot collected materials for hospital use which were then sent to the war zones in Europe. People donated money and gifts and hundreds of volunteers made up dressings, bandages and splints which were then packed and dispatched abroad. In one week alone, 2,848 articles were sent. The names of the ladies who served tea to the workers were recorded in the local paper!

Picture D - THE WAR HOSPITAL SUPPLY DEPOT. This plaque on the wall of no.8 Causeway (to the left of the museum) commemorates the many women who helped make up supplies for hospitals in Europe during the First World War.

The distinctive, green-painted building next door is Horsham's Museum (E). Also known as Causeway House, it was the home of a wealthy merchant in the 16th century. It consists of 3 floors, with the top two floors jettied, or extended, over the street. In those days, the tax each household paid was based on its ground floor area, so a jettied first floor increased the space inside without any increase in tax! If you go inside you can clearly see that it is a large timber-framed building, but in the 18th century the timbered front was plastered over as was the fashion of the day.

The railings (E1) in front of the museum are covered in jagged spikes. When this was a private house, they discouraged passers-by from peering in.

Picture E - HORSHAM MUSEUM is a beautiful medieval timber-framed building. It has twin gables and an unusual window design. The museum also houses the Visitor Information Centre.

Picture E1 - The spiked railings in front of the Museum were to deter snoopers, as this was once a private house.

The Museum, which is free, has displays of local history, housed in over 26 galleries. The fascinating but rather ghoulish 'Crime and Punishment' area (F) includes a replica of a cell from the old county gaol. It was a model prison when it was built, with separate cells for each inmate, the first of its kind in the country.

Picture F - CRIME AND PUNISHMENT is one of the exhibits in the Museum. This display shows an enormous padlock and a formidable set of keys, together with handcuffs and colourful truncheons. Most of these came from the County Gaol which was pulled down in 1845.

Another display shows that those found guilty of murder were sent to the gallows or burnt at the stake. In 1735 a prisoner was 'pressed to death' under the combined pressure of a 400lb weight (about 184kg) and the executioner who lay on top! Horsham was the last place in England to carry out this gruesome torture. John Weeks of Fittleworth was accused of murder and robbery but refused to speak. To 'encourage' him to defend himself, he was subjected to 'pressing', in public, but unfortunately died in the process.

If you walk through the Museum's pretty garden, you will come to several outbuildings which house carriages and carts, a collection of bicycles and a lovely old fire engine. The 'Hen and Chickens' (G) was the nickname given to a bicycle adapted from the familiar pennyfarthing. It was invented by a Horsham man, Edward Burstow. Unfortunately, it did not work very well, so it never went into mass production.

Picture G - THE HEN AND CHICKENS can be seen in the Blazing Saddles room at the back of the Museum. This 'Pentacycle' was invented by a Horsham business man. It was intended for tradesmen and tried out by the Post Office but it was not a great success.

Walk a little further down the Causeway on this side and you will come to numbers 11, 12 and 13 Causeway (H). Number 11, with brown weather-boarding, and the pink timber-framed number 12, was one house called 'Hadman's' which was once occupied by a tailor called Henry Patching. When he died, in1614, an inventory of his possessions showed that he had 12 rooms including a shop with 6 shelves and a 'shoopborde'. (This was probably a hinged counter).

Picture H - NUMBERS 11, 12, 13 CAUSEWAY. You can walk right through the charming pink timber-framed building into a narrow twitten called Morth Gardens.

The entrance to the narrow alleyway called Morth Gardens goes right through number 12. If you walk along this twitten (a Sussex name given to a narrow alley with high walls) you can look back to see the interesting gables and roofs of these houses (I). If you peep over the high wall, on the left, you can see some Victorian summer houses.

Picture I - MORTH GARDENS. As you walk into the twitten (a narrow walkway with high walls) look behind you to see these two gables with their decorated barge boards and unusual hanging tiles

A little further down are two attractive white cottages (I1). Morth Gardens is named after John Morth, a carpenter, who built these cottages for his daughters. This footpath marked the boundary between church land to the south and Horsham borough to the north.

Picture I1 - PRETTY COTTAGES in Morth Gardens. The one on the right is covered in white weather-boarding.

Turn right at the end of the twitten into Denne Road and walk down past the Drill Hall. The Hall was built by the officers of the 4th Battalion of the Royal Sussex Regiment and the Royal Observer Corps for both active and retired soldiers. It was a popular venue for dances during the Second World War, having the largest sprung wooden floor in Sussex. A Heritage Trail sign on its walls gives more information.

Just past the Drill Hall is the Lychgate of Denne Road Cemetery (J). The land for this Victorian cemetery was acquired when the graveyard surrounding St Mary's Church became full. You can walk through this tranquil place, part of which is managed as a nature reserve. One area is a 'peace garden' where different trees represent the allied countries of the Second World War. Several well-known Horsham residents are buried here. When this cemetery was full, another, in Hills Road, was opened.

Picture J - LYCHGATE, DENNE ROAD CEMETERY. Just past the Drill Hall is this Victorian cemetery. The inscription reads 'All that are in the graves shall hear His voice and shall come forth'.

Turn right into a little cul-de-sac called Normandy (K) where you have a fine view of St Mary's Church with its lovely east window. Normandy was probably named after a Norman French brotherhood of monks which was attached to the church and helped look after the poor and destitute. The almshouses on the left are a reminder of this connection to the church. A priest's house, an early vicarage, stood between the almshouses and the church at one time.

There was a bell foundry in Normandy in the early 17th century, probably to your right in an area known as Bell Field. 90 of these bells were still in existence in Sussex churches well into the 20th century.

The tall church spire is 156 feet high (nearly 48 metres). It twists and leans to the south-east. One night, in 1615, there was a tragic accident during a storm. The church tower and one of the five bells was damaged and Elie Stroode, a maid, 'was killed with thunder at ye belfery doore'. Luckily for us, the church now has a lightning conductor!

Picture K - SAINT MARY'S CHURCH FROM NORMANDY. To the left of the church are almshouses. These replaced old cottages which were, at one time, an old workhouse. The fine church spire leans slightly and is covered with no less than 50,000 shingles (wooden tiles).

Passing through the graveyard to the left of the church will lead you to some pretty gardens laid out by Councillor Nella Laughton in 1926 as a memorial to her husband and the men of Horsham who died during the First World War. Keeping left here will take you to a bridge which crosses the river Arun (L).

If you walked left from the bridge, along the river, you would eventually come to Chesworth Farm Nature Reserve. This is one of several beautiful wild life habitats managed by Horsham District Council. Nearby is Chesworth Manor, a medieval moated farmhouse. Catherine Howard lived at Chesworth as a teenager. She became Henry VIII's fifth wife when she was twenty and he was fifty but she was beheaded two years later for indiscretions with young men more her own age.

A walk through the gardens would take you to the site of the old Town Mill which later became Prewett's Mill.

Picture L - THE RIVER ARUN. A walk through the churchyard will bring you to a bridge which crosses the river. Paths lead from here into the countryside and to the Cricket Field.

Retrace your steps to the church and walk round the tower until you come to this 12th century doorway (M) which is near the main porch. The church was founded during the reign of King John but was largely replaced in 1247. In the 19th century, the walls were leaning badly and massive restoration work was carried out. The tower and this doorway are part of the original Norman church, about 900 years old.

Picture M - 12TH CENTURY CHURCH DOORWAY. Just to the right of the main entrance you will find this door. Note the rounded Norman shape and the beautifully-coloured sandstone.

If you go inside the church you can see the tomb of Thomas, Lord Braose (N). This type of monument is sometimes known as a 'funeral helm' with the medieval knight lying in his armour over his tomb. His two young children died soon after and so they are buried with their father in this tomb.

After the Norman Conquest, Sussex was divided up into a number of strips of land from the coast which were called 'Rapes'. Thomas was a descendent of the first Norman Lord of the 'Rape of Bramber', William de Braose, whose castle was at Bramber. Horsham lay within this Rape and Thomas owned Chesworth Manor, so it was natural for him to be buried here.

400 hundred years ago, the interior of the church looked very different. There were pews with high backs and galleries were built to accommodate the expanding congregation. Places in the pews were 'to let' and the front seat cost 1s. 2d. (15 pence) for the 'roome for their lives times'.

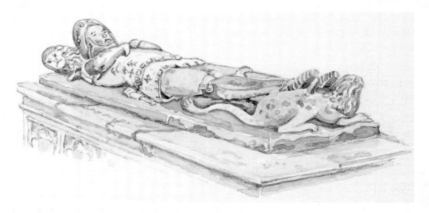

Picture N - THE DE BRAOSE MONUMENT. You can pop into the church to view several fine monuments. This effigy of Thomas, Lord Braose, who died in 1395, shows him in his Knight's armour and lying with his head and feet on lions.

Inside the church there is a memorial to Horsham's most famous resident, the poet Percy Bysshe Shelley. Shelley was born at Field Place, a large country house in Warnham. His wife, Mary, also gained literary fame for her horror story about Frankenstein. Shelley was drowned at sea in Italy. His body was cremated and his ashes buried in Rome. As a committed atheist, it is a bit unusual that he should have a memorial in the church.

Returning to the churchyard, you will have noticed that you are walking on some enormous paving stones (O). Some of these are old gravestones, some taken from the inside of the church when it was restored. These sandstone slabs were dug locally and, if you look carefully in the churchyard and in Pump Alley, you may see ripple marks on some. Many millions of years ago, when dinosaurs were roaming the area, these were laid down as sand bars, probably in a giant estuary that stretched from here to the English Channel and to France.

Picture O - PAVING STONES. If you look at some of the slabs in the churchyard, you can see ripple marks. You are looking at the action of water flowing over sand. These features were formed over 100 million years ago.

The most interesting tombstone is the one on the left by the gateway. This is usually known as the 'Tomb of the Black Princess' (P). Helena Bennett was born at Lucknow, India in 1772, the daughter of a Persian Cavalry Colonel serving in India and an Indian lady. At the age of six, she was briefly married to a local maharajah but he was 72 and died before the marriage was consummated! She was therefore a princess for a while. In 1787, aged fifteen, she married a French soldier of fortune called Benoit de Boigne, by whom she had a son and a daughter. They later came to England, but when de Boigne inherited his father's estate and the title of Count, he deserted poor Helena, returned to France and married a French lady. Helena lived the last 50 years of her life in a cottage in Colgate.

Tradition has it that her grave faces north-south so that she could be buried Muslim fashion, facing Mecca. However, as the graveyard

Picture P - THE TOMB OF 'THE BLACK PRINCESS'. As you leave the churchyard to rejoin the Causeway, you will see a grave which lies north-south, unlike the other tombstones which are all east-west. This is the grave of Helena Bennett from Colgate. Her story is quite extraordinary.

was closed in 1852 and she died in1854, it is more likely that she was squeezed into the last remaining space by the gate, hence the unusual alignment. You will see that she has a cross on her gravestone.

The criminals who were hanged in Horsham were buried in unconsecrated ground in the south-west corner of the churchyard, in unmarked graves with no tombstones.

From this point, you can see a charming pale yellow house called 'Flagstones' (Q). The side of the house overlooking the churchyard is made of brick and little round-shaped hanging tiles. In Georgian times this would have been a fashionable 'improvement' to the original timber-framed façade. The bricks and tiles would have been made of clay dug in the Horsham area and fired on the spot.

Picture Q - FLAGSTONES. This lovely house has an attractive uneven Horsham stone roof and unusual carved barge boards. The date, 1615, may refer to rebuilding or alteration as the house is early 15th century.

If you look at Flagstones' roof, you will see that it is covered in large slates known as Horsham Stone (R). They are adorned with various mosses and lichens. This is the same sandstone as the paving and gravestones, but the slabs were split to form tiles. Nevertheless, they were still very heavy and needed massive timbers to support them. They were fixed to the rafters by drilling a hole through which was driven an oak peg, a nail or even a splinter of bone. Horsham Stone was dug from shallow pits some of which can still be found on the hill above Nuthurst village. The Romans also knew the value of Horsham Stone as some was laid along Stane Street.

Picture R - HORSHAM STONE ROOF ON FLAGSTONES. Many houses in the Causeway are roofed in large slabs of sandstone, extracted locally and therefore known as Horsham Stone or Slates. You can see that the largest slates were laid on the bottom of the roof where there is greatest structural support.

Walk back up the Causeway and look at numbers 18, 19 and 20 (S) which are on your right hand side. The grey flint house, number 18, was an alehouse, a shop tavern. The writer Hammond Innes lived in this house as a boy in the 1920s and attended the local school, which was at number 8 Causeway, next to the Museum. The white house, numbers 19 and 20, may have been a Lay Brothers' House

Picture S - NUMBERS 18, 19, 20 CAUSEWAY. These charming white weather-boarded cottages originally belonged to the Church. At Number 18 Thomas Picke, a barber-surgeon, ran his old family business in this house until he died in 1681.

attached to the church. These were non-ordained members who carried out church duties but could not preach or take communion. They also worked as servants in the kitchen, laundry and gardens.

The brick house, number 15, was called the 'Six Bells'. Just under the eaves you can spot a fire plaque and ladder eyes (T). In case of fire, your insurance company sent their own fire engine and you paid for this service. However, by the 1720s, Horsham parish had its own fire engine.

Picture T - FIRE PLAQUE AND LADDER EYES AT NO. 15. If you look under the eaves, you can see 'eyes' for attaching ladders in case of fire. The fire plaque showed to which insurance company one belonged. The company sent its own fire engine.

Picture U - MINSTRELS. This is a handsome tile-hung house which was once three houses. The one nearest the church is of a 'continuous jetty' type, with the first floor built out over the pavement.

On the other side of the road is a much-photographed house known as Minstrels (U). This lovely house has a beautiful Horsham Stone roof and the front is covered in hanging tiles. In the 1880s, this was three different homes. Furthest from the church were two shops: Charles Vaughan, Bootmaker and W. Randall, Breeches Maker.

Picture V - HEWELL'S MANOR HOUSE. Just past Church Barn, with its semi-circular windows, is this imposing building. Built in 1704, it was the headquarters of the RSPCA for many years until 2001 when it was converted into stylish apartments.

Opposite the Museum and behind high walls is 'Hewell's Manor House' (V). This fine Queen Anne house was built for Nathanial Tredcroft over 300 years ago. It was a grand estate, with fountains and the grounds led right down to the river where Sainsbury's is today. Unfortunately, his great-grandson, Edward, got heavily into debt to the local solicitor and money-lender, Henry Padwick, who took over the house in exchange for debts. It later became a private school, was the headquarters of the RSPCA for 28 years until they moved to Southwater and is now luxury flats.

Walk back past the Town Hall until you come into the Carfax. Old documents show that it was a large open space called 'Scar Folkes' or a place that was 'scarce of people'. This seems the likely derivation for the curious name 'Carfax'. Originally, this big, empty space was where markets and fairs were held, but it has gradually become occupied by permanent buildings.

On the right, as you enter the Carfax, you will see the former King's Head Hotel (W) which has been unoccupied for a number of years but there are plans (2009) for it to become a restaurant. It was an important coaching inn where travellers could rest and change their horses on their way between London and the coast. In Victorian times Horsham seems to have had a lot of pubs, possibly over 50, about one for every 100 residents! (The population was 5,765 in 1841).

Picture W - KING'S HEAD HOTEL. This old coaching inn was in existence in 1665. It was the Tax Office from 1852 until 1881, hence the lettering on the wall.

Picture X - SAINT MARK'S CHURCH. In the corner of the Carfax stands the old church spire, in strange juxtaposition with the modern insurance buildings around it. It is now the headquarters of Horsham Volunteer Bureau.

The modern day Carfax is a mainly pedestrian area with attractive seating and floral displays and limited access for vehicles which must keep to 20mph. In one corner was St Mark's Church (X) which was demolished to make way for a large insurance company. The spire is all that is left. This corner of the Carfax, which joined North Street, was also known as Gaol Green because a gaol and the gaoler's house stood here. These buildings are still there behind their modern shop fronts.

Two prominent features of the Carfax are the War Memorial and Bandstand (Y). The original war memorial was built to commemorate those who died in the First World War and stood near the bus stop. It was moved to its present position in 1992 and enlarged to show the names of those who died in the First and Second World Wars. The Victorian bandstand was built in 1892.

Picture Y - WAR MEMORIAL AND BANDSTAND. The Memorial is surrounded by iron railings of poppies. The Bandstand, with its decorative blue-painted ironwork, is a popular venue for concerts.

Also in the Carfax, towards Swan Walk, you will find the Stocks and Whipping Post (Z), a reminder that punishments used to be meted out in public. Someone guilty of crime could be whipped, branded or placed in the stocks where they could be taunted by the crowds. Another horrid practice was that of bull-baiting where a bull was tethered to a ring and goaded by bull dogs. This was said to sweeten the meat which was then sold in Butcher's Row, now Middle Street. The ring can be seen in the Museum.

Picture Z - STOCKS AND WHIPPING POST. These are in the centre of the Carfax and are a reminder that punishments used to be carried out in public. These are replicas, the originals can be seen in the Museum.

This completes the main walk. There are many places in and around the Carfax where you can find refreshment. You may then like to take a look at some of Horsham's very fine sculptures (see second map). Until 1990, Horsham did not have any public works of art. There are now several and they are a very popular feature of the town.

The Sculpture Walk

MAP TO SHOW POSITION OF
SCULPTURES

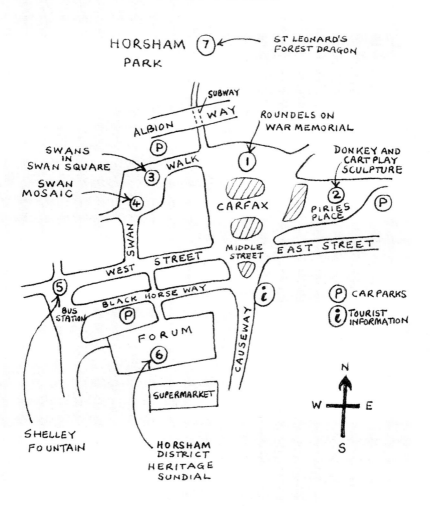

HORSHAM ⑦ ← ── ST LEONARD'S FOREST DRAGON
PARK

SUBWAY
ALBION WAY
ROUNDELS ON WAR MEMORIAL
Ⓟ
SWANS IN SWAN SQUARE → WALK ③
SWAN MOSAIC → ④
①
DONKEY AND CART PLAY SCULPTURE
②
PIRIES PLACE
Ⓟ
CARFAX
SWAN
MIDDLE STREET
WEST STREET
EAST STREET
⑤
BUS STATION
BLACK HORSE WAY
Ⓟ
FORUM
ⓘ
CAUSEWAY
Ⓟ CAR PARKS
ⓘ TOURIST INFORMATION
⑥
SUPERMARKET
SHELLEY FOUNTAIN
HORSHAM DISTRICT HERITAGE SUNDIAL

N
W ─┼─ E
S

The Celebration of Life Roundels (1) are in the middle of the Carfax on the back of the War Memorial and both children and adults can enjoy identifying the many plants and animals depicted in the three sculptures. These roundels were created by the sculptor Edwin Russell.

Picture 1 - CELEBRATION OF LIFE ROUNDELS. On the back of the War Memorial, in the Carfax, are 3 fascinating sculptures celebrating life in air, earth and water. You can identify at least 20 animals in this roundel.

The Donkey and Cart Play Sculpture (2) is in Pirie's Place. This delightful sculpture, which is designed to be climbed upon, was created by the nationally recognised sculptor, Lorne McKean. Lorne is married to Edwin Russell. They live and work in Surrey.

Piries Place is named after William Pirie who built a row of 15 cottages here which became known as Pirie's Alley. He was the headmaster of a school called Collyer's which was in Denne Road. Collyer's moved to Hurst Road in 1893 and is now a large sixth form college.

Picture 2 - DONKEY AND CART PLAY SCULPTURE. Children and adults alike delight in this charming piece. It features Mr Pirie, headmaster of Collyer's from 1822-1867. He was often to be seen driving himself about in his donkey and cart.

The Swans in Swan Walk (3) were also created by Lorne McKean to form a centrepiece for the Swan Walk Shopping Centre.

This beautiful bronze sculpture shows three swans about to land. Tiny fountains over the webbed feet and tail of the lead swan give the impression that it is just hitting the water.

Picture 3 - THE SWANS IN SWAN WALK. This beautiful work of art is by celebrated sculptor Lorne McKean. The swans were removed in 2007, but reinstated in 2009 after a massive public protest which was supported by the County Times.

The Swan Mosaic (4) is also in the centre of Swan Walk. Two flying swans are depicted in a circular design. The swans are a reminder of the Swan Pub which was at the West Street entrance of Swan Walk. It was demolished to make way for the new shopping centre which was opened in 1976.

Picture 4 - SWAN MOSAIC IN SWAN WALK. Constructed in the Italian style, it is worth stopping to admire the many tiny tiles which make up this attractive work.

The Shelley Fountain (5) is at the bottom of West Street. Also known as 'Rising Universe', it is an unusual water feature which is spectacular when it rises up and drops 7 tons of water in a single cycle. It was created by the sculptor, Angela Conner. It forms a focal point for this area, with seats and flower beds. Horsham is beautifully decorated with flowers, shrubs and trees and the charity 'Horsham in Bloom' have helped it win regional, national and international awards.

Picture 5 - SHELLEY FOUNTAIN or RISING UNIVERSE. Bold, but controversial, sculpture erected in 1996 to celebrate the bicentenary of Horsham's most famous poet, Percy Bysshe Shelley.

Horsham Heritage Sundial (6) is situated on the large open space known as the Forum which is between Blackhorse Way and Sainsbury's. It was unveiled by her Majesty Queen Elizabeth II in 2003. This impressive sculpture is the work of husband and wife team, Lorne Mckean and Edwin Russell, together with Damien Fennell, and with historical information provided by the curator of Horsham Museum, Jeremy Knight.

Picture 6 - HORSHAM HERITAGE SUNDIAL is on the Forum and is a unique 3-dimensional, bronze ring. Look carefully and you can see that many aspects of Horsham District's history are represented. A Horsham time capsule has been buried in the stone plinth.

A short walk will take you to Horsham Park with its beautiful old trees, duck pond, lawns and St Leonards Forest Dragon (7) in the middle of a fascinating little maze. Here, you can find out more about local legends. There is also a large children's playground, the 'Pavilions' (swimming pools and gym) and a bandstand in the Park, together with a scented garden and a welcome Conservatory Café.

Picture 7 - ST. LEONARD'S FOREST DRAGON is to be found in the centre of a little maze in Horsham Park. The scaly skin of this mythical beast is wonderfully sculpted.

Glossary

Architectural terms used in this book

Barge board A board, made of wood in old buildings, which runs under the roof. At the gable end it was often carved to make an attractive feature.

Crenellation The top of a wall, often on a castle, with gaps, originally for firing through. Also called battlements.

Gable The triangular upper part of a wall between the sloping ends of a ridged roof.

Jetty The area where the upper floor projects beyond the ground floor so that it sticks out over the pavement.

Lychgate A roofed gate to a churchyard, formerly used as a temporary shelter for a coffin.

Shingle A thin light rectangular tile, usually of wood, laid with others in overlapping layers to cover a roof or wall, but most often used on church spires.

Timber-framed Many medieval buildings were built with a framework of stout timbers, hence timber-framed. The walls were then in-filled or clad with other materials such as stone, brick or plaster.

Weather-boarding A timber board that is fixed with others in overlapping horizontal rows to form an exterior cladding on a wall.

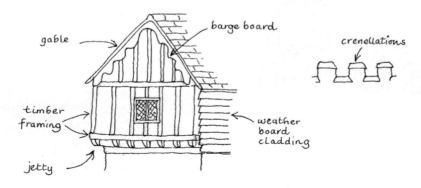

CAUSEWAY

Acknowledgements

I am most grateful to Jeremy Knight, Curator of Horsham Museum, for his constructive criticism of the text and for sharing with me his impressive knowledge of Horsham's history. Matt Williams designed the layout of the book and gave me friendly and professional support. Many thanks also to Jenny Fowler and Bernice Middleton who read the text and offered valuable suggestions, and to my husband, Mike, and my daughters Jackie and Amanda for their help and patience in the long preparation of this book. Lastly, my thanks are due to my mother, Margarett Maddocks, now aged 90, who has badgered me for many years to produce this book before 'it's too late'!

Suggestions for Further Reading

For a lively account of Horsham's history:-

Susan Haines, ***Horsham - A History***, Phillimore & Co Ltd, 2005.

For more information about Horsham's old houses:-

Annabelle Hughes, ***Horsham Houses***, Phillimore & Co Ltd, 1986 and other books by the same author.

For those who are interested in Horsham's geology:-

Roger Birch, ***Sussex Stones: The Story of Horsham Stone and Marble***, Roger Birch, 2006.

For the definitive view of the history of Horsham:-

Jeremy Knight, ***Horsham History, Volumes 1, 2, and 3*** (4 and 5 in preparation), Horsham District Council.

Websites:-

www.horshammuseum.org
www.horsham.gov.uk

About the Author

Patricia Hall was born in Eastbourne, Sussex, the daughter of an architect. A zoology graduate, she taught biology at Steyning Grammar School for nine years where she was also Head of Science. It was here in the picturesque town of Steyning that she started painting and married her husband Mike. The arrival of two daughters prompted a change of career and for the past 30 years she has developed a second successful career as an artist and publisher.

Although she has no formal training in art, she has sold over 75,000 limited edition prints and many people will be familiar with her greetings cards and calendars of Sussex.

'Armchair Walks in Sussex - Horsham' is her first venture into writing and illustrating a book. She plans further titles in this series featuring other towns and villages in Sussex.

Patricia and her husband lived in the Horsham area for twenty years but have now moved to Ferring near Worthing where they brought up their young family many years ago.